I COLOR TO KEEP FROM CHOKING YOU

BY: MICHELLE JENKINS

I Color To Keep From Choking You

Adult Coloring Book for Adults on the Edge

Copyright 2018 by Michelle D. Jenkins

All rights reserved in all media. No part of this book may be reproduced or transmitted in any form by any means, electronic or mechanical, including photocopying, scanning and recording, or by any information storage and retrieval system without written permission from the publisher, except in the case of brief quotations embodied in critical articles and reviews.

Published by Montsho Publishers
customersupport@montshopublishers.com

ISBN: 978-0-9679795-4-0

DEDICATION:

To my son Christian better known as my surprise from GOD at forty and the reason I need this book most days :-)

Sometimes Life Sucks...

I Color To Keep From Choking You.

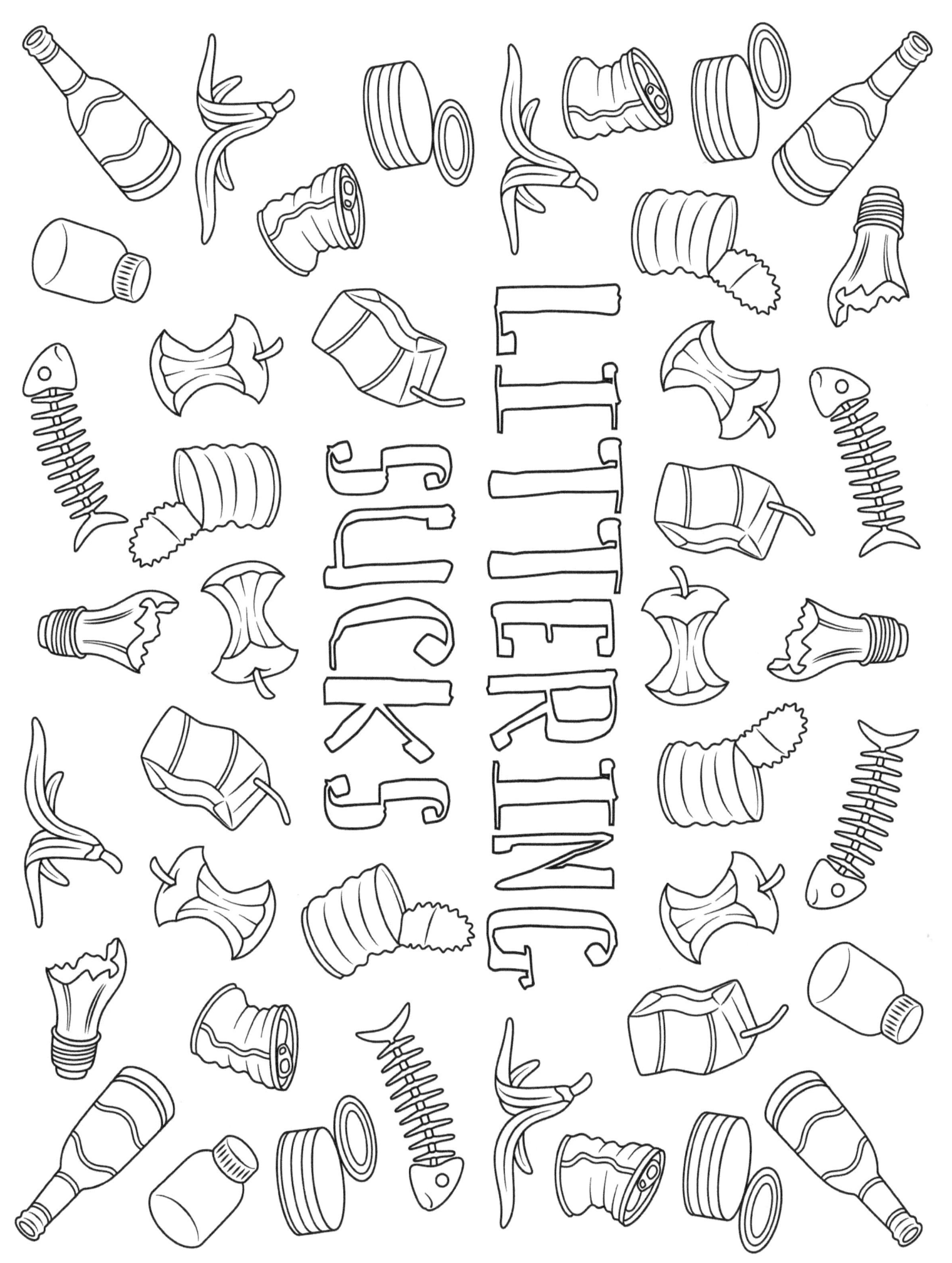

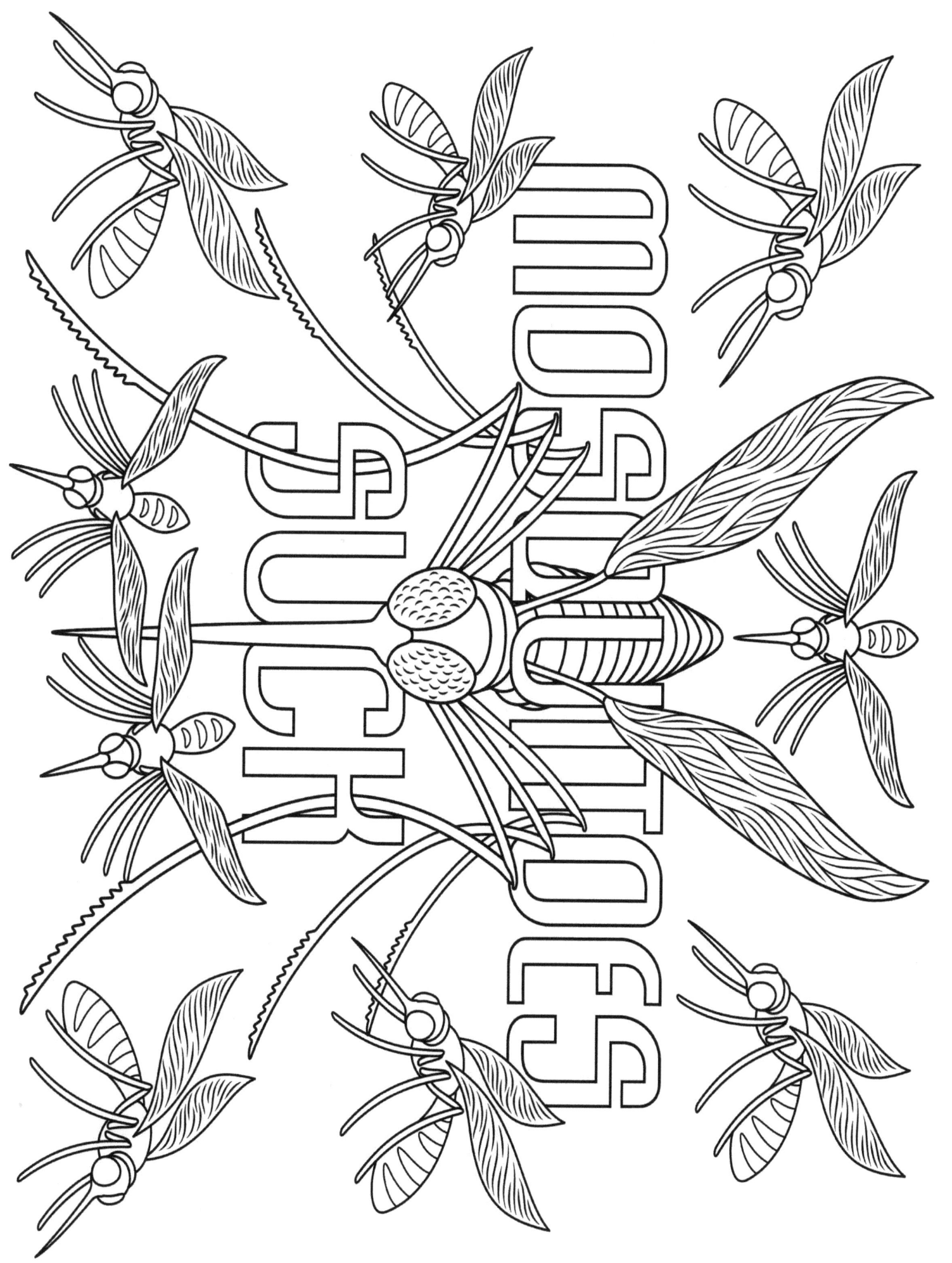

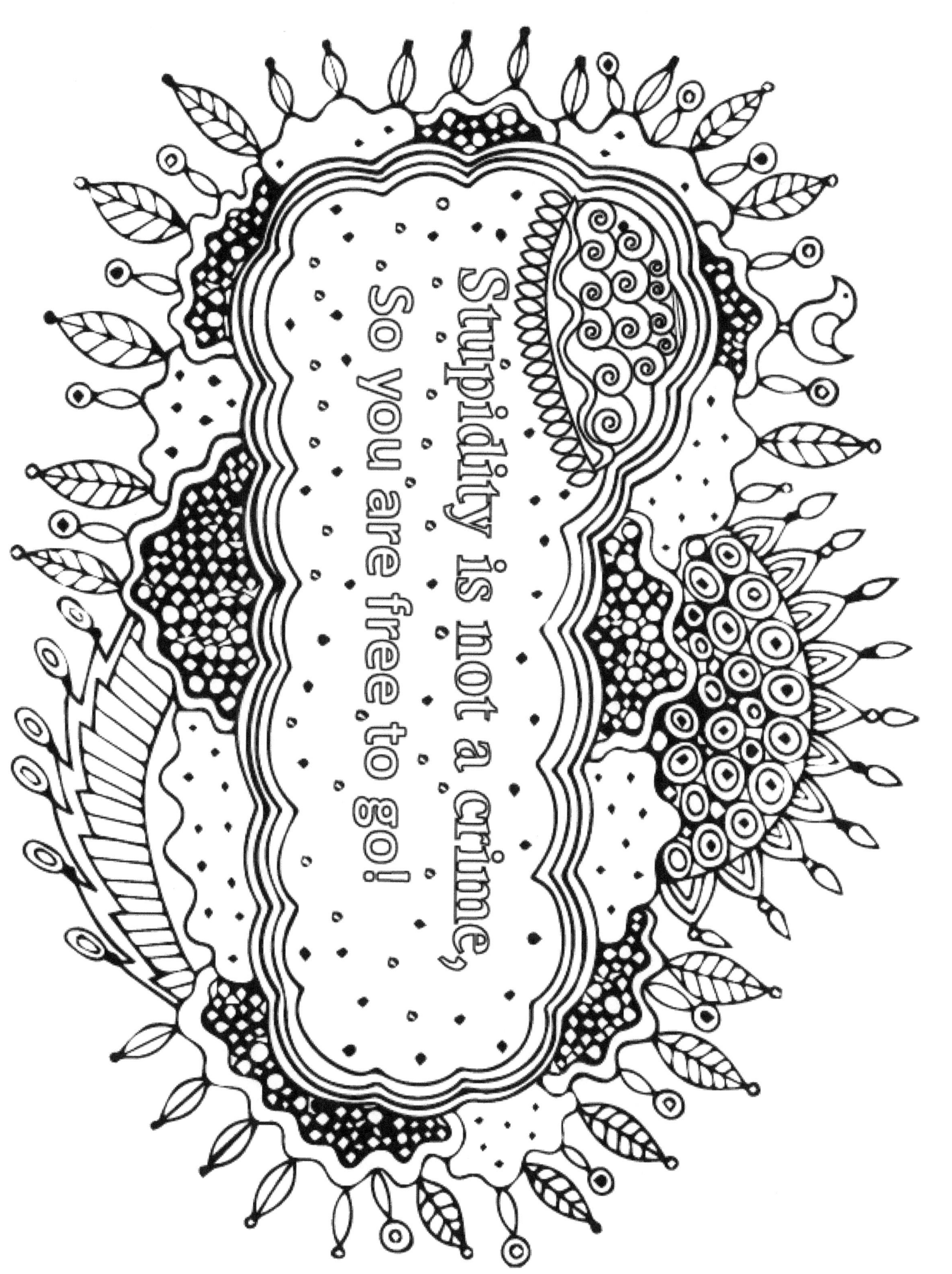

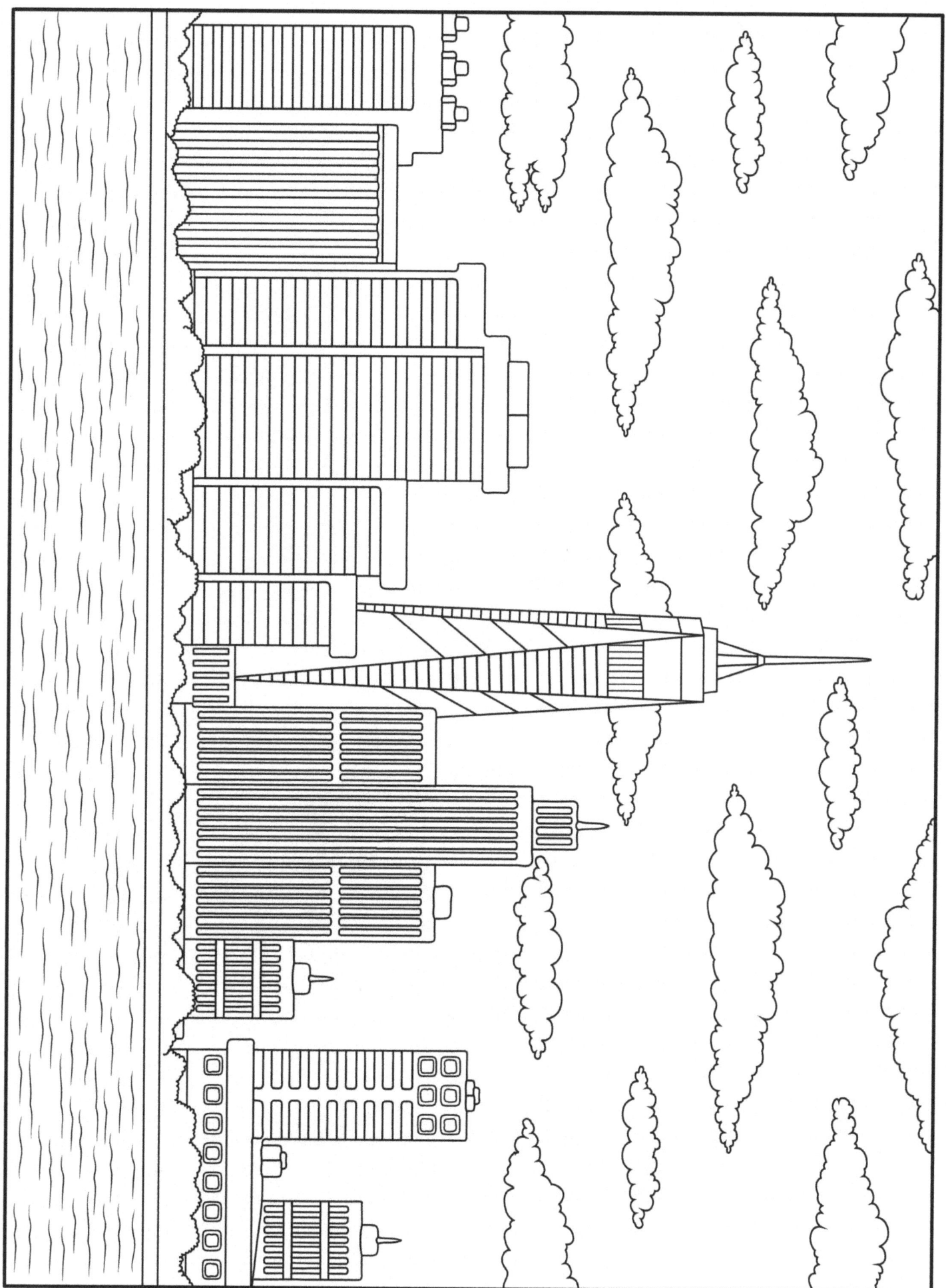

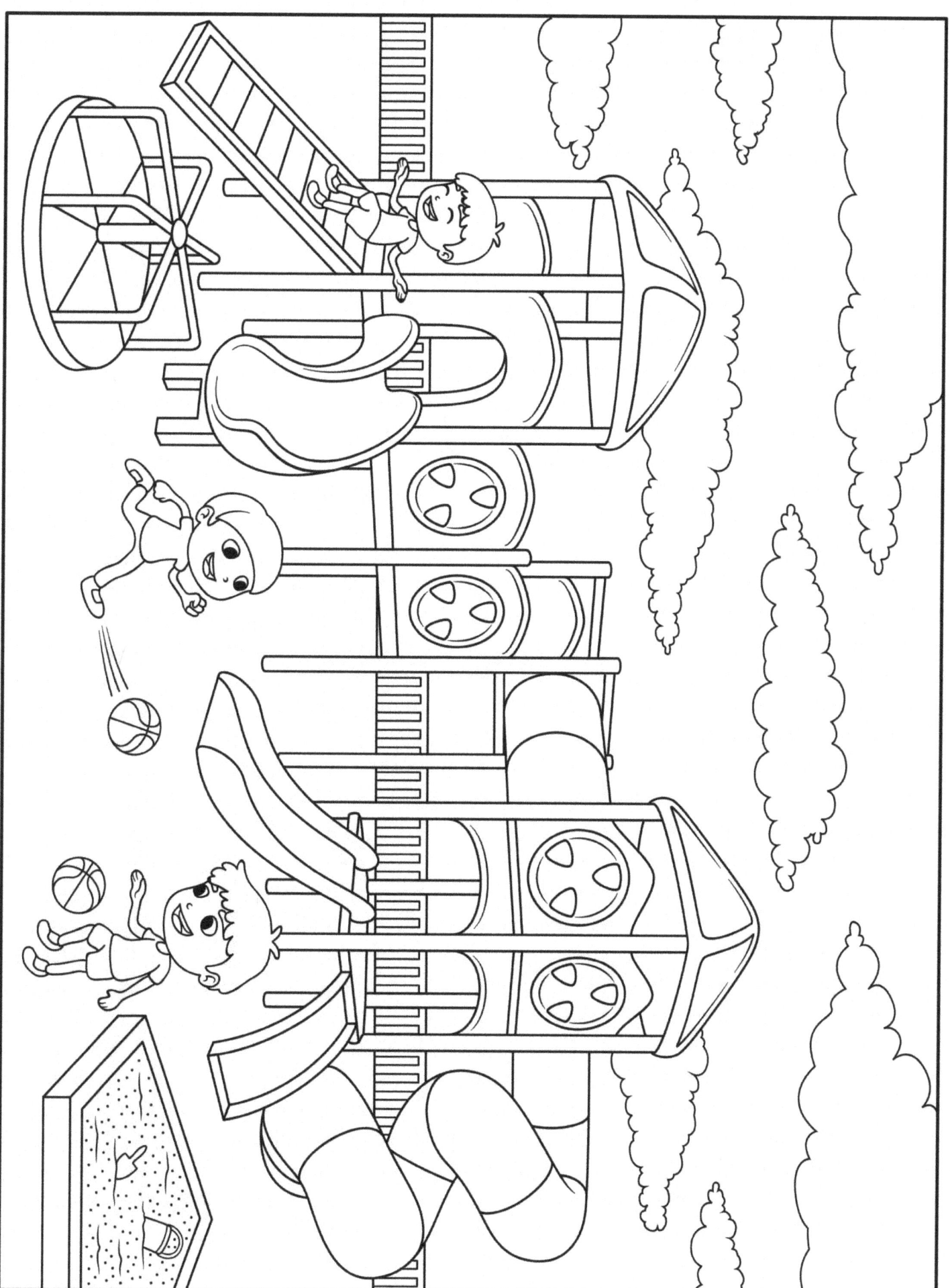

I hope you enjoyed this book as much as we did creating it for you. We are working hard to continue to come up with designs you will love. If you have any designs you would like us to add to some of our upcoming books please send us an email.

Or if you just want to let us know what you think about the book you can do that also. Again thanks for your purchase and look for more books coming soon!

customersupport@montshopublishers.com

Copyright 2018 Michelle D Jenkins

More books by Montsho Publishers:

1) Simple Prayers for Everyday Life Situations - 978-0967979533
2) Slightly Twisted Words of Wisdom and Other Funny Sayings - 978-0967979526

www.ingramcontent.com/pod-product-compliance
Lightning Source LLC
Chambersburg PA
CBHW080940040426
42444CB00015B/3385